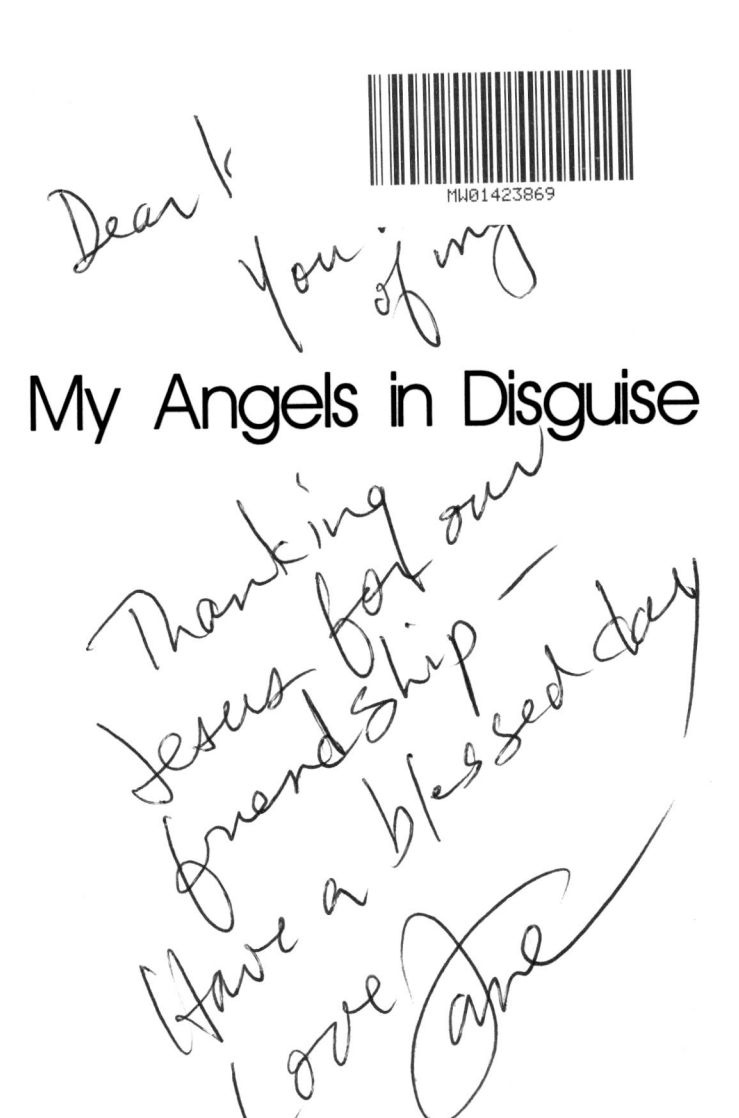

My Angels in Disguise

Dear K

You of my

Thanking Jesus for our friendship

Have a blessed day

Love Jane

My Angels in Disguise

*How God Helps You
in Times of Trouble*

Jane Blakewell

ISBN 978-1-60920-129-6
Printed in the United States

© 2018 Jane Blakewell

All rights reserved

Library of Congress-In-Publication Data

API
Ajoyin Publishing Inc.
P.O. Box 342
Three Rivers, MI 49093
www.ajoyin.com

Cover photo credit: Angel Steusloff

No part of this book may be reproduced or transmitted in any form or by any means, electronic or mechanical—including photocopying, recording, or may any information storage and retrieval system—without permission in writing from the publisher or author, except as provided by United States of America copyright law.

Please direct your inquiries to admin@ajoyin.com

Contents

Foreword 1
Introduction 2

Chapter 1 *All About Angels* 4
Chapter 2 *Angels and Scripture* 9
Chapter 3 *The Gift of Music* 13
Chapter 4 *Servanthood* 16
Chapter 5 *My Parents and Tom* 19
Chapter 6 *The Teen Years* 23
Chapter 7 *Angels in College* 26
Chapter 8 *The Riverside Angel* 28
Chapter 9 *Early Marriage Memories* 31
Chapter 10 *Angels at Church* 33
Chapter 11 *In the Swimming Pool* 38
Chapter 12 *Angels as Physicians* 40
Chapter 13 *Four-legged Angels* 45
Chapter 14 *My Support Groups* 48
Chapter 15 *Christopher and Elizabeth* 51
Chapter 16 *God's Purpose Revealed* 55
Chapter 17 *The Little Angels* 57
Chapter 18 *My Beloved Roger* 61
Chapter 19 *God's Great Love* 64
Conclusion *On Looking Back* 66

Foreword

I BELIEVE GOD ORCHESTRATED a perfect plan for my protection before the world was created. To God be the glory for great things He has done. I would like to thank the many people, whom I call angels, who walked with me throughout my life and will continue to be faithful to the end.

God put angels on assignment for me, whom He chose from the very beginning. These wonderful, precious friends of God became my family prayer warriors from day one. They had the desire to uplift and encourage my parents, my entire family and me. They gave us hope and assurance that blessings would follow.

I am dedicating this book to the angelic family members, friends, professionals, and to those I was totally unaware of, as accidents and illnesses continued and how special they were in keeping me from harm. I can continually boast in the Lord, sharing God's love with anyone who will listen. Psalm 9:1 reads, "I will praise you, Lord, with all my heart; I will tell of all the marvelous things you have done."

Introduction

I AM WRITING THIS book because I feel an urgency to share my joy to all who were prominent figures throughout my life. *Sink or Swim?* was my personal testimony, but I never really understood the significance of those who helped me. Attitude is gratitude. All of us have a choice, and choosing to stay afloat was my only choice.

It is totally amazing to me how many precious people have been involved in my life. Some I am aware of and many I never saw while in desperate need. I don't remember if I ever showed any gratitude or appreciation for their continual prayers and for rides to any destination whenever necessary. Many times, I was in my own little world and overdosed on too many drugs to stop the ongoing seizures.

As God created and planned my life, He was very aware I would need special caregivers who would serve Him with gladness and who would look forward to giving their love away freely. They would choose to stand with me because they desired to do it. Difficult testing would continue, and their hands were there for me to hold onto. They encouraged me by saying, "We can jump this hurdle together." They had so much love in them and believed God would turn the tide and become the victor.

"Angels watching over me" is the theme of this book. Many of them appear in the form of friends, family, and strangers who just walked up and said, "Count me in!" Seizure activity caused me to be absent mentally many times, so my imagination could only grow wild as to who may have been there as my accidents and falls were unpredictable. It will bring great joy to greet them at heaven's pearly gates. I will stand amazed as I recognize who they were. His timing was always perfect, as they appeared every time I was in need.

God has purposes and reasons for all He creates. Angels are blessings He designed to comfort us and help us when in need. They can be heavenly beings singing glory to God or earthly beings like your next-door neighbor. It will be amazing to find out just how many angels you may have entertained throughout your life without ever knowing it.

When we leave our earthly world, we may meet one of the faithful ones who happened to be at the right place at the right time because God planned for them to be on duty. We are being watched and people can react and respond differently. We may be surprised one day just how many lives we could have touched and were never aware we'd done anything.

My story revolves around this thinking: I had and still have angels on duty 24/7. Each one of us has a role to play while on earth. God will call us home and we may walk up to many we recognize and some will be complete strangers.

Angels are prayer warriors who play important roles in our lives and odds are we will know who they are. We can have smiles on our faces, saying, "Remember when?" We will then have the opportunity to embrace in love.

Chapter 1

All About Angels

THE GREEK WORD for angels is "aggelos," and the Hebrew word "malak," both meaning, "messenger, either human or celestial, sent from God to bring tidings; commissioned to perform a purpose." They act decisively in fulfilling God's will in the world. Angels around us, beside us, and within us. Their wings wrap around us and let us know we are loved. God created angels to guide, protect, and strengthen us. More importantly, angels always are praising and glorifying God! They are all around and transport blessings to us throughout our walk on this earth.

Angels are everywhere, but often, people aren't even aware of their presence. Even though you can't see them, angels are around you this very moment and will often leave signs to reassure us that they are not only with us, but also that all is well. Angels were sent down to earth to learn certain things about the human condition and to guide humans on earth.

These angels are usually Spirit Guides in training, or Spirit Guides who have been sent back to earth to learn more and heal others. You can encounter them anywhere at any time. Often, the chance encounters with these angels have the power to change your life. While some angels can know and feel they are different and are often aware of their spiritual duties, others seem to forget and have a hard time managing their life on earth.

Are you interested in knowing if you've been visited by an angel? If so, it might be time to take a closer look at the signs around you. Here are a few signs that angels may leave and how to spot them.

Angels will often come while we sleep because we are relaxed and receptive. While you dream, your guardian angel may step into the dream, to make personal appearances, maybe as a friend or teacher. The angel may just be sending you thoughts and feelings as you sleep.

Sometimes you may receive an urgent phone call and an exact time, or maybe angels intervened somewhere along the way, making them think of you, just at the right time or giving them clarity or wisdom to offer you advice you need. Angels may send messages in the sky. This includes rainbows confirming their presence with you. It can be really cool when rain is nowhere in sight!

In my story, many angels and workers among us are here to help and guide others through life. Angels remind us of their presence, helping us through difficult times and letting us know they are with us. Even if we aren't aware their presence, they are there. Angels will always find a way of alerting us.

Angels remind us to seek the best in ourselves at all times. Integrity is a virtue. Angels wish to remind us to act as role models to help without expectations of anything in return. They remind us to lighten up in our lives and have a little fun! Laughter is always healing. They add to the magic of fun and joy associated with the celebration and festivities. They will not back down and won't accept surrender as an option.

Angels were standing with God cheering and praising him at the world's creation. They were there when Adam fled from the Garden of Eden and also while Noah was building the ark. They are here now as our daily lives are blessed.

Angels are our heavenly co-workers and friends who have served the Lord day and night for over 5,000 years. The Bible specifically states an awareness of them over 300 times. These references are found in over 34 books of the Bible, from Genesis to Revelation.

There are many angel warriors and fellow servants ready to help us at all times. Hebrews 12:22 says, "an innumerable company of angels." In Revelation 5:11 it states, "I heard the voice of many angels round the throne and the number of them was ten thousand times ten thousand and thousands of thousands." The cosmos is brimming with millions of angelic beings who exist solely to do His will.

We need to be aware that angels were assigned to help us fulfill our destinies. They were shown what God actually had in mind as He created us individually, and there is no identical person like you or me anywhere on this earth. Angels are ready to assist us when troubles seem hopeless in our own eyes. They don't just show up, but only as God assigns duties for them, because they hearken to His call at all times.

Knowing there are angels provided as our days on earth continue, produces faith and confidence in God. We can get relief and be strengthened, rescued and protected by His angels. They are supernatural, celestial of pure spirit, superior to humans in power, beauty, wisdom, goodness and serve God doing only His bidding. By nature, they are spiritual entities and thus not subject to limitations of the flesh.

Angels are very intelligent, wise and clever and do not quit until they complete an assignment. They have emotions and wills that are divine. They help us know how to trust

God and how to have courage to face what the enemy meant for harm. They minister to saints, execute judgments, lead sinners to Gospel workers, watch over our children and grandchildren. They help to re-gather the Jewish people all around the world and bring them back to their homeland Israel. They impart God's will and bring answers to prayer.

They are joyful, powerful, mighty and best of all--nothing is impossible for them! They carry God's divine glory, and are obligated to hear His word and bring it to pass. They have wills, can make decisions quickly, and they serve God by choice with great passion and love. Job 38:7 says, "The morning stars sang together and all the angels shouted for joy!"

When their assignment requires it, they can appear in our world and look like us. They are sinless, wise, offer direction and protection and will go to war on our behalf. They help us to achieve and be prepared as God opens doors for us to witness and share God's love. They will not do the work for us. They can teach us to understand our purpose, help release our potential, for we have abilities inside us that we may not be aware of.

So, our eyes need to be opened daily to follow where they lead us so we can bless others. They could easily direct us to a neighbor next door, a co-worker at work, or a cashier in a grocery store! God works in mysterious ways! Where are angels today? Everywhere. They love as God loves. We can be sure we are surrounded by angels as we are on our spiritual journeys. This hierarchy among spirit beings was established before the world was created.

Cherubim, are beyond the throne of God and are guardians of light and the stars. Their divine light filters down from heaven and touches our lives in many ways. They are considered the elect beings for the purpose of protection. Angels continually hovered around me as my story unfolds.

Seraphim serve as caretakers of God's throne and continuously sing His praises. There are only four of them and their bright light coming from their beings is too bright for anyone to look upon them.

It has been proven that Christ has been the subject of more songs, music, stories, literature and art than any other subject in the history of mankind.

God offers His pure and selfless love through the use of His angels. Angels protect and direct us, reveal information and minister to believers. They assist us in our deliverance from sin and eternal death. The gift of God is eternal life and is brought about by faith in Jesus.

Christ rules over His holy angels as well as the fallen angels. One third of the angels created chose to follow Satan and are referred to as demonic angels for they behaved foolishly and proved to be untrustworthy. God's angels are on our side and far outnumber the demons, principalities and powers of the devil. The influence of Satan and his followers will meet their end when they are consigned to the lake of fire God has prepared for them.

Be encouraged by the number of God's angels who are eager to help us fulfill His plans.

Chapter 2

Angels and Scripture

THE PSALMS GIVE blessings and peace. Psalm 34:7 shares, "The angel of the Lord encamps all around those who fear Him, and delivers them." God performed many deliverances in healing, both mentally and physically. His deep compassion and love has been forever strong. After learning who I am in Christ, and who Jesus really is, salvation became reality. Healing would be a miracle if I believed, and would come in His time.

Psalm 91:9-10 says, "If you make the Lord your refuge and dwelling place, no evil shall harm you nor will any disaster come near your dwelling." You are secure when God is in control.

Verses 11-12 continue, "For He shall give His angels charge over you to keep you in all your ways and they will lift you up and protect you." Verse 14 is His promise, "because he has set his love upon Me, I will rescue him; I will protect him because he has known My name. Verses 15-16 continue, "He shall call on Me and I will answer him; I will be with him in trouble; I will deliver him and honor him. With long life I will satisfy him and show him My salvation."

Angel friends invited me to join them at a new church. God's people sang scripture while putting it to music.

Psalm 34:1-4 shares, "I will bless the Lord at all times, His praise shall be continually in my mouth." Singing His word brought joy. Verse 4, "I sought the Lord and He heard me and delivered me from all my fears." As I grew closer to Jesus, fear disappeared. Total trust developed through it all.

Isaiah 43:2 speaks directly to me. "When you pass through the waters, I will be with you; and through the rivers, they shall not overflow you. When you walk through a fire, you shall not be burned, nor shall the flame scorch you." God had angels surrounding me all my life as trials continued. Many involved water and He just held on tight. I never drowned in the pool or in the river nor did I suffer a burn while fighting cancer and hip replacements because of His tender loving care.

II Corinthians 12: 9-10 says, "My grace is sufficient for you. My strength is made perfect in weakness. When I am weak, then I am strong." Throughout my seasons of infirmities, friends and family people whom I now call angels, were always there ready to help me take another step. They encouraged me to keep walking a straight line, looking only to Jesus which gave me hope, and taught me to desire to know Him as my best friend.

I enjoyed inhaling scripture and memorizing it by singing choruses. Music, once again, brought healing. The words became alive and brought joy overflowing. Even today I can be reading areas of scripture and just because I heard it once in a certain melody, it came back like lightning!

1 Corinthians 10:13 states, "God is faithful and will not allow you to be tempted beyond what you are able and will also make a way of escape that you will be able to bear it." God knew every day what could actually happen to me, so He prepared people, whom I call angels, who would desire to keep me from danger.

I needed hope, wisdom and the ability to learn how to give Jesus my life. I needed His blessing so He could do His will, without me getting in His way. I found many angel friends in Bible studies who had sweet gentle spirits, listening ears and a desire to reach out in love. My angels in disguise were sharing their lives and time, to help me stay afloat. They never gave up praying with me and for me.

God has knowledge to what we must be exposed to as we journey through life. He knew exactly which angel would be perfect for my needs, to help keep my head held high. God's chosen angels were able to share their thoughts, prayers and locate scripture they knew that would help me increase my faith.

Psalm 103:19-20 states, "The Lord has established His throne in heaven and His kingdom rules over all. Praise the Lord, you His angels, you mighty ones who do His bidding, who obey His word. Praise the Lord, all His heavenly hosts, you His servants who do His will."

Psalm 34:19 reads, "Many are the afflictions of the righteous, but the Lord delivers him out of them all." When you become a child of God you are righteous in His name. But God is always faithful and did come to my rescue whenever I cried out... and even when I didn't. Angels were always on the lookout 24/7.

Romans 5:3-5 states boldly, "We glory in testing, knowing that testing produces perseverance; and perseverance, character; and character, hope. Now hope does not disappoint, because the love of God has been poured out in our hearts by the Holy Spirit who was given to us." Angels in my life continually surrounded me with love and gave me hope to keep fighting.

In short, angels are messengers, warriors, worshippers, protectors who get direction from God alone. What a blessing from God!

Angel friends were aware when I needed comforting. They just showed up at our door, knowing I needed a shoulder to cry on and love flowed through them to me. God put the desire in their hearts to fulfill His call in their lives. I could trust God, for He always had my needs fulfilled. God sometimes brought either complete strangers or close friends to our door, when loneliness enveloped me and prayer was necessary.

Psalm 103:20 says, "Praise the Lord, you His angels, you mighty ones who do his bidding, who obey His word." Angels are here for a purpose and were created just for us because of God's incredible love.

Chapter 3

The Gift of Music

I THINK EVERYONE READING this book has heard the lyrics: "angels we have heard on high, sweetly singing o'er the plains…." I believe angels enjoy singing so I think music is not only important to angels as they praise God but in my case, music was vital to my survival.

When I was unconscious following my diving accident at age 14, the doctors said music kept my mind alive. My mother played a piano and sang hymns. My friend and neighbor, Ellie, also played the piano and sang my favorite songs. When I returned to school following my recovery, I attended my first, introductory class and it was a music class, taught by Mr. Rodby, the school music and choir director. He later suggested I join his Viking choir.

In particular, I loved the musicals by Rodgers and Hammerstein, Lerner and Lowe and Gilbert and Sullivan. Memorizing words to the songs became a game to me. The more I did it, the more fun it became. The words of musical melodies are medicine to the soul. God restored my health through music assisted by angels in disguise like my mom, Ellie and Mr. Rodby.

From the very start, God used singing, because it would become prominent in my life. Putting scripture to music made worship easier because it came naturally. The brain is truly amazing and healing would be restored as music played continually throughout my coming back to life.

Schools now have music therapy as a major. It was never considered an option when I started college. Music has played a major role as seasons of my life fanned out. Later I was introduced to beautiful spiritual songs from the book of Psalms. A great way for God's word to be magnified in my life.

When they put the book of Ecclesiastes to music, I sang the scripture, "to everything, there is a season.... A time for every purpose under heaven. A time to be born, a time to die…. A time to weep, a time to laugh…. A time to mourn, a time to dance… A time to keep silence, a time to speak… and my favorite is verse 11, "He has made everything beautiful in His time."

Psalm 100 is my favorite one. "Make a joyful noise unto the Lord, serve the Lord with gladness and come into His presence with singing, know that the Lord is God. It is He who has made us. We are His people and the sheep of His pasture. Enter into His gates with thanksgiving and into His courts with praise. Give thanks to Him and bless His name." While I was able to sing the Psalm in high school, I had no idea who God was or that He had actually brought me back to life. As an adult now, I am getting to know the Great I Am as a close friend.

Music is a potent treatment for mental healing. It has positive physical effects and can reduce heart rate, blood pressure and relieve stress. The message in a lyric could actually reach more people than all therapy in the world. God used music therapy to awaken my soul. Fun lyrics help us think positively. Research suggests that the brain responds to music almost as if it was a medicine. What exercise is to the body, music is to the brain. The power of music can inspire physical movement, like swimming, dancing and water ballet.

God uses music today to keep me in good physical shape, uplifted and full of joy. We have a great Creator. Seasons in life came alive as music was used to anoint and uplift my Spirit. I learned to see all of life as a blessing as friends (angels) walked me through life as my caregivers.

Learning to be positive while struggling was not easy. God sent angel friends who had experienced hard times who taught me to be an overcomer. Hope developed as I chose to reach out to those in need, instead of focusing on my trials. These angels had their hands full, but they desired to please God and I was always blessed because of their love.

Chapter 4

Servanthood

LOOKING BACK AT my early years, there were many outstanding people who were just waiting to be used by God. All were fighters who never stopped praying, knowing only God could make things work together for good.

Many Angels assisted me, never realizing what they were capable of doing until the door opened. They willingly said yes and became servers doing whatever was necessary to keep things moving forward. Servanthood is a gift. When I was sick from the diving accident, our family was totally amazed as people came to our home asking how they might assist us, never questioning anything. They just said yes.

Servanthood brings joy and restores life to the hurting soul and uplifts the caregiver.

While in the process of healing, feelings and emotions flew by me with questions as to why it was necessary to continually have people on duty just for my safety. This can cause needy people to quit asking for help because they thought they were interrupting others' lives. They sadly chose to end their lives. I had a few friends in the epilepsy and cancer support groups who had decided they had had enough of life. Unworthiness caused depression and then became suicide. They chose to stop living, which was not God's plan.

The Bible has a great deal to say about serving. The main theme of the Bible is the servant of all: Jesus. "For the Son of Man did not come to be served but to serve, and to give His life as a ransom for many." Our love for God will be expressed in our love for others.

Serving others is the very essence of ministry. We are called to be servants for the glory of God. Living is giving; all else is selfishness and boredom. Rank is given to you to enable you to serve those above and below you. Let's serve others by serving Christ. God served us by sacrificing His Son on the cross for our sins. We can serve others by giving the gospel and our lives to them.

We should want to serve God because we know Him, and want to be like Him. His entire life was centered on serving God, by teaching, healing, and proclaiming the Kingdom (Matthew 4:23). He came not "to be served but to serve" (Matthew 20:28).

Genuine service can't be separated from love. We can go through motions of serving God, but if our hearts are not in it, it is meaningless. Serving should be natural and full of love. When you become aware of His grace and mercy given to you, your response is to serve Him. We can only give away what we have received.

Our goal through servanthood is to give God the glory for the great things He has done. The power of Jesus is on display in the lives of those who have traded selfishness for selflessness. Believers should know that when we speak and serve directly on behalf of God to others, that He gives us the ability and strength to do it. When we direct glory to Jesus versus ourselves, we stand out in a crowd and others will want what we have. They will desire to examine the life changing nature of a relationship with Jesus and the desire to learn all about faith.

I had total dependence on people while ill and throughout many years of my life. When you have been given a gift that keeps on giving, you desire to return it.

That is why it became easy for me to reach out and touch anyone I saw in need, because it had been done to me all my life. It wasn't anything I needed to be taught or even shown how to do. It was natural. Love flows out selflessly, and it flows continually and never stops.

There is a song I sang at campsites and at church. It starts, "It only takes a spark, to get a fire going.... That's how it is with God's love, once you've experienced it, you want to pass it on." I love shouting it from the mountaintops, the Lord of love has come to me and I want to pass it on.

Chapter 5

My Parents and Tom

HAVE YOU EVER thought of your parents as angels? Your brother? Well, it is possible. My parents were special people who put family first and made sure we knew we were loved unconditionally. We were blessed with joy as our close relationships grew stronger as we got older. Our dad was a hard worker in a retail business which required many long hours, weekends and holiday away from home.

Mom was a great cook and invited many close friends to taste her delicacies, so our house was full of cheer and entertaining others was a great priority in their lives. I never had a close relationship with either of them until later in life. My brother Tom and I got along well and we enjoyed time growing up together.

Mom and dad would be spending more time praying and learning all about God's Word after my diving accident. They had many sincere friends who were firm believers in God saying continually that nothing was too hard for Jesus. They prayed for hours and uplifted each other daily. They grew closer to each other as they drew closer to Jesus. They encouraged my parents to hang on to their faith, which would be established as they continued their journey forward. They would eventually see me blossom and come back to life again.

My mom was always singing and playing the piano. She was very creative and was always amusing friends with great comments that made everyone laugh. I joined her and we had fun memorizing words to new and old songs and beautiful hymns. Music was always in our lives and hearts. She was also a fantastic artist, trained at the Chicago Art Institute, using almost any kind of drawing materials. She loved using charcoal, oils, water color or pastels. She did portraits of many friends and family.

I will never know how they were able to handle the stress that continued daily as I remained unconscious so many months. Hearing what they actually talked about would have been devastating for me to hear and very hard to handle emotionally. My brother Tom filled me in with a few surprising answers to my questions, since my parents never discussed my illness, nor did I ever ask them.

As mom grew older, she said she didn't want to discuss it or she didn't remember. I believe that after my brother had experienced my long illness and dad fighting throat cancer, all of this became a deciding factor as to why he chose to pursue a career in hospital administration. He was very successful in several large hospitals in the greater San Francisco area.

There are many blank spaces in this part of my story. So, it is a mystery who that angel may have been in the woods where the pool was located that day in July 1962. Looking back, I think if my friends had actually watched and seen the blood everywhere after the shallow dive, they would have called their parents and taken me to the hospital before the deep infection would overtake my body. So, I truly have no idea if I crawled on my own or if there was a guardian angel at the poolside. Who knows, I may meet that angel someday in heaven!

My three Jewish doctors were angels in disguise getting wisdom from above for our family and me. Though they were not totally aware of the possibly high brain damage, they were willing to fight with all their might and do anything they could to come up with answers to just keep me alive.

God would be their guiding angel, giving them wisdom so they could learn different techniques and get more ideas from specialists nationwide. Back in 1962, they had no modern medical technology or any computer systems like we have now. For example, my brother said I laid with ice on top of me and below me to help keep my high fever under control.

God would be blessing these angel doctors. They would experience seeing a miracle come to pass, because of the many angel prayer warriors, never relenting, until they saw and experienced the victory. The doctors could see no hope, but after three months, the high fevers broke and the grand mal seizures ceased as I came back to life. My parents were warned that though the seizure activity ceased when I awoke, the seizures could return again in the future and possibly in another form.

I am looking forward to greeting these doctors and nurses who chose to walk the extra mile to keep me alive to the end, who I never saw nor thanked. They were gems who really loved their chosen career, their patients and families.

Caring friends of my parents were their right-hand angels. I was gifted to chat with a few recently and they shared a few stories. They were angels who stepped into the scenes to support and relieve my parents. At 14, I had the mental state of a two-year-old. My brother told me I had to be watched 24/7, because I now was strong enough to run out into the street having no idea what I was doing. I thank God daily I have no memory of being ill, as I slowly came back to life. God had precious friends chosen before time began. I admire their ability to stand strong in severe hardship. Jesus was their anchor.

I really have no idea who most of the angel caregivers were back then. These wonderful people would all be blessed at seeing the end of the story that they all had played an important role in. I chose to be married in my hometown of Flossmoor, Ill., and they were able to witness what God had put together and had done in my life since the severe illness.

Not only had I graduated from high school and college, but was now marrying a man who loved me. The guests experienced seeing me shine like the morning sun as I walked down the aisle with my father and his big smile. My mom had a few close friends who opened their homes for wedding showers and others who prepared food and served cake after the service. My mom and dad had the joy of seeing love overflow all day and had the ability to relax and enjoy the festivities without lifting a finger. God had prepared everything perfectly.

It will really be fun greeting the people, angels, who were in charge of planning the parties and wedding, as heaven's gates open. They will all be blessed 100-fold because of their obedience and strong desire to be servants of the most-high God.

Chapter 6

The Teen Years

MY MEMORY EMERGED more quickly than predicted by doctors as they stood amazed seeing God's Hand in my life. My brother Tom shared ideas and filled in answers to many questions I had never asked when I was younger. Now as an adult, the puzzle pieces that were missing needed to be unleashed.

I know I went to a child psychologist in Chicago after returning to high school with questions about why old friends were now a year ahead of me. She was an angel who was able to give me peace and must have convinced me on what had happened. I had to take a train to downtown Chicago by myself and I've been told that often I got off at the wrong stops.

My parents had to learn to cut the apron strings, as they worked with the psychologist, and wait to see what God had in mind. I really have no idea what this doctor did for me, but I now had freedom and was about to fly. God brought in some new friends to walk by my side and they chose on their own to spend time with me. They knew I was confused but loved me through it all. It was a great big step. People could actually see how God was working and were amazed at how things quickly fell into place.

I have no memories of ever hoping I'd get better, because I was unaware I had been sick. I truly do not remember anyone ever telling me that it was a miracle I was alive. It seemed as I just went back to school with a year missing.

This psychologist and all the teachers at the high school were miracle angels. They chose to share their time and had great patience as they worked with me. They wanted to walk me to and through classes, knowing I'd need help initially and then they also could let go. I remember very little about my high school years.

I'm sure I will hear stories when I meet up with all of them in heaven. It was a blessing to be around grateful caregivers as my life unfolded. It would have been fun watching how God had planned my recovery and all the work He went to finding these blessed angels to watch over me as I healed.

The first class I truly remember with joy was the Viking choir. I had to try out, and Mr. Rodby accepted me. We sang music of all faiths and the performance was recorded initially on an LP album. The record had many scratches from listening to it over and over again. I was thrilled getting our performance that had been put onto a CD.

I remember memorizing every word and note as we practiced daily. Many were in different languages and one was in Hebrew! Psalm 100 was my favorite psalm put to music, as it shares the wisdom that we should all "make a joyful noise unto the Lord and to serve Him with gladness." Psalm 23 also was put to music and lets us all know that the Lord is our Shepherd and there is no other.

Mr. Rodby was really the only teacher who remained in my memory out of all my high school teachers. Amazing what a blessing, an angel, he was to me by admitting me to the choir. Putting scripture to music and singing it over and over was a perfect teaching tool.

Because of my dad's throat cancer and loss of his voice, my parents had to move to Wisconsin so he was able to work with his new handicap. That meant they had to leave the Chicago area prior to my senior year. They needed wisdom from God as to who might be available and could handle any problems if and when they arose. Finding someone to help would mean I wouldn't have to start my senior year at a strange new school.

I was blessed abundantly by being invited to stay my last school year with Evelyn, a good friend of my parents. She just wanted to give my parents relief and this opened a door to bring freedom to my new life. No one truly knew if I would be able to handle school and my parents living a few hours away. All were amazed how easily this transformation worked without any difficulties occurring.

In high school I remember a few close angel friends, Chris and Becky. They stood by me and were willing to walk the extra mile through all the wiles of a new school and new classmates. We went to basketball games and enjoyed being together. I had two big dates in high school, which were "turn-about" dances where the girl asked the boy.

Years later I would see Bob, the violinist, at our 50th class reunion. Most of my classmates remembered me more than I remembered them. About 165 students came and many saw me, asking me if I remembered choir practice and water ballet shows we were in.

Most of the students in my high school class were college bound, so I decided to join them. I found a school in Wisconsin, where my parents now lived. I chose UW--Eau Claire, where I would meet many new friends, many of whom we still see today. I chose to major in elementary education and psychology. After graduating from high school in 1967, I moved back to my parent's home which was in Lake Geneva, Wis.

Chapter 7

Angels in College

I WAS FINALLY ON my own. God had put new life in me and where it would take me was all in His Hands. My roommate in my freshman year had her hands full with me. I needed to mature quite a bit. I enjoyed my classes and new friendships and had no difficulty studying, writing papers, getting good grades or taking exams. It all became very natural. There were many challenges and hardships, but I walked through it all. The friends I met while student teaching and beyond, all have played important roles in my life.

I never have had any bad memories or disappointments about classes I'd chosen or wishing I had decided on another major. The teachers were outstanding and I was developing new relationships with friends who enjoyed the same activities and skills I enjoyed. Dating was not really important to me. The large campus was located on the beautiful Chippewa River, so walking, climbing stairs, and getting to classes on time was a challenge. No one owned a car. The campus was beautiful being located on the river.

Summers were always fun to relax and work in our family retail store, to help with college costs. In my second summer my cousin's boyfriend wanted to come to the resort town to see her but he had no car. So, he asked Roger Blakewell, an angel in disguise, if he'd drive to Lake Geneva.

Roger agreed to drive and we met in my uncle's store. After that weekend, my cousin never saw her boyfriend again and I have been married to Roger 46 years. God doesn't make mistakes when He moves. Our meeting was not by accident. God knew I would need someone strong and able to make decisions immediately when problems arose. My aging parents would not be able to handle situations in my life ahead.

After dating over a year, he decided to take a leave of absence from his job and finish college. We graduated a week apart and got married. Two little girls who came to the beach where I life guarded for two summers were our flower girls in our June wedding.

A beautiful wedding day with a church full of my praying angels who cared for me while coming back to life. I am sure they stood amazed at God's healing ministry.

In 1971 I was a substitute teacher in a new, experimental year-round school system in the Chicago area, and Roger's job involved too much traveling and distance driving. It was not the job he desired. A writing and editing position opened up a few years later in Wisconsin. I was not thrilled about the move because teaching jobs were few so my future was in jeopardy. A close friend I knew well was concerned about me and we would later find out why.

Roger was the star angel of the college era and remains number one 46 years later. It is a blessing that no one has a clue about their future and what it may hold. Only God's grace would hold our precious marriage together because we would be facing many adversities we would not be prepared for. No one has any ideas what God has planned.

Chapter 8

The Riverside Angel

WE NOW LIVED in Wisconsin and I was not happy to be there. Roger enjoyed the challenge of his new job. The town had no need for substitute teachers and my days seemed empty. I took a lifeguard supervisor job at a pool for the summer for something to do. Occasionally I would see bruising in different areas of my body, but had no memory of ever falling or bumping into anything, so I just ignored it.

We had one car which Roger needed to get to work. I hadn't driven anywhere by myself in this new town and had no idea where the pool was to get to my meeting. God was aware I'd need angelic intervention that special morning. I hadn't asked for it, but God was in control.

On my way to work on that quiet Saturday morning in June I had a seizure and drove into a river. As I was awakening from experiencing a new kind of seizure, I saw two eyes just staring at me with his arm motioning me to roll down the window.

Talk about angelic intervention! When I was totally aware something was really wrong, I was frightened and panicking. We had a two-door car and the tiny back window had a small handle I was able to grab onto and roll down a bit. How he was able to pull me out of the tiny window of a nearly immersed car is totally beyond my comprehension! That alone was a miracle!

The doctors in Chicago had told my parents 12 years earlier, seizures could return in another form. They said the grand mal could change into a complex partial seizure. The victim is totally unaware a seizure is about to occur and when awakening from it, there is no awareness of time passing.

But now I was soaked, my car was under water and all I could do was panic, because I would be late for my lifeguard meeting! Amazing! A man, an angel, was there at 8:00 a.m. and witnesses told me he literally pulled his car off the road and jumped into the river. Where did he come from?

All I remember was telling the officer I had to get to my job or I'd be fired. Did I ever thank the man who jumped in and saved my life? No, my mind was not functioning after the seizure. God wanted me safe, secure and ready to tell the world He gives His angels charge over us, no matter where we are or what we're doing. God had stepped in and knew my need and provided this angel and I was unharmed. Grace and mercy overflows.

We did try to thank this young man, this angel, but his family said by phone he had died. Died? How could he? Not from the river experience certainly. Was he my guardian angel again who stepped in when I needed him and then stepped out again?

Truly a mystery. God only knows. I will look forward to meeting this angel who brought me to safety. I can only hope I can say how grateful I am to anyone God plants along my path, ready to go all the way, just to make sure I'd be safe and protected.

I have questions for God as to just how I got out of the pool unharmed and made it through a deadly illness and now a car accident. I just think about all the people it affected in each situation and the troubles it brought on as I healed each time. It would have been so simple for Him to just have taken me to heaven after the shallow dive. What was His purpose for any of these near disasters?

The missing puzzle pieces seem to be fitting together more easily. I can see more clearly how it actually brought people together praying, waiting and watching for miracles to happen and seeing God as He really is. The Great I Am. He works in mysterious ways.

The many people who were involved as I was healing throughout my life have been touched by God as He let them serve, which brought them joy as they persevered. In the end, it actually changed their lives, opening doors they had not seen before to be able to reach out and desire to care for others. I want to tell the world of His gracious love because I experienced His love through others ministering to me. Psalm 9:1 says, "I will tell of all the marvelous things you have done!"

Chapter 9

Early Marriage Memories

I NOW WAS TOTALLY aware that my life had changed forever. Any plans I had for teaching were over. Substitute teaching never happened because driving or seizures could happen anytime and stress would be a major problem. My freedom was taken away and now my self-worth was pretty much gone.

Roger had to leave daily for work and sometimes needed to be out of state on business. It amazes me how he could concentrate, knowing I was alone and could be in danger anytime. He was successful in everything he did, and chose to hold on, no matter what the cost. He breathed great love into me.

We had only been married three years and had no children. He would provide for me in sickness and in health. We really didn't know each other that well, but we were both fighters who chose to grow closely together. Roger himself had been deathly ill at age 14, and God introduced us on a blind date. That's our God! He knew that we could make it and we'd need each other for many years.

I needed something to keep my days filled. We decided a baby was a great idea! Doctors were shocked that we even imagined we'd be able to handle caring for an infant. The medications I was on could cause serious physical problems for a growing fetus. Approximately nine months later, our son Chris was born. A medical miracle and healthy from day one.

After six weeks hormonal changes took place, I experienced a severe breakdown. Roger was the one who suffered more than I will ever know. I was hospitalized three months, while his parents cared for Chris. They were angels in disguise also and I really have no recall of ever thanking them, which I regret. I could make up excuses, like that I was overdosed on too many seizure medications, but I was really living in my own dream world. It amazes me that I was able to function as a mom and wife. What God puts together, no man can separate.

God moved us to a perfect neighborhood with a house which was close to a few families of His own choosing. We had no idea what would happen. I would need a close friend and He knew just who I needed.

A few years later God blessed us again, this time with a healthy girl, Elizabeth. Chris was now four and our family was knitted together in love. Our children were special and caring for me as they grew up. I think I was a good mom and did all I could do under the circumstances. No physical damage to the children or me occurred during a seizure because all of us were under Jesus's mighty Hand. We were under His covering. Looking back and seeing His continual care is quite incredible. Our new neighbors were aware of our needs and kept watching out for any problems that could occur and they'd reach out in love.

We were blessed later in life to be able to bring joy to Roger's mom, after her husband passed away. My parents lived in Florida and with my seizure problem, I could never travel to see them. I feel I knew his mom more than my own. It was great she lived closer. Caring for her in later life made up for the many times in my younger life that I said nothing for all she'd done for me.

Chapter 10

Angels at Church

LOVE SHOULD FLOW out of any church. However, at the church we attended, people were not friendly. And it wasn't for the lack of trying. I believe they were afraid of my seizures and had no idea what to do nor had any desire to help. Roger suggested I socialize and get to know them. Having nothing to say to strangers did not interest me.

I loved all the beautiful hymns they sang and tears came to my eyes singing beautiful songs about the Lord. It brought memories about high school and singing about His goodness back in a new way. It was always a very formal service. Our children went to their private school and had been in children's choir many years.

I never was aware of how people reacted when a seizure occurred. Years later I witnessed seeing a friend from an epilepsy support group, experiencing a seizure. She walked around, dug around in her purse, and slowly came out of it. Roger walked into the room and told me I responded as she had. I'm so glad I never knew what people saw when my seizures occurred. No wonder people were afraid and wanted to run away. They would actually try to help, not really understanding what they could do to assist me. It was simply best for everyone not to panic and wait the seizure out.

Days seemed to last forever, especially in winter when I was trapped inside with nowhere to go. I was blessed by being invited to help with sing-a-longs at the nursing homes or assisted living facilities. I walked the halls and brought wheel-chaired patients who desired to sing and get out of their small rooms. I turned the pages for them and sang with everyone. We did it weekly, so I easily memorized three or four stanzas of many hymns!

Angel Joyce picked me up faithfully and we sang, read scripture and entertained many for at least an hour each week. It brought joy and smiles to many lonely people. It made me feel worthy and that there was a reason God brought Joyce into my life. Helping hurting people gave me peace and I was able to understand they really needed fellowship and hugs.

Ministering to people in need became easy for me, because people had given that gift to me for many years. Joyce also started a National Day of Prayer, where about 10 of us chose to get together and pray for the nation and the leaders. She provided rides for me for many years. I had Bible studies at our home to meet people and study His Word.

God opened a huge door when I met an angel named Cindy. She had seen my deep need for fellowship and acceptance from people who had compassionate hearts. She asked Roger if she could take me to her church on Sunday night. Absolutely! I was elated because someone actually cared to spend time with me.

We walked in and I was greeted and given hugs from everyone. They offered me rides to church weekly and most were full-time moms. Love overflowed directly on me. Their hearts were full of Jesus. The Spirit was alive as they all sang songs of praise lifting up holy hands and clapping to the beat of the music. All in honor of the Great I Am.

Their joy filled the sanctuary and I didn't want it to stop. There was an altar call for new believers and also prayer for healing. I ran forward and asked Jesus to be the Lord of my life. I was anointed with oil and prayed for by many who laid their hands on me, asking Jesus to hear their cries for healing of my seizures.

I assumed medication that wasn't working or surgery which I didn't qualify for were the only possibilities for my healing. I believed God could heal me when I truly believed in faith that nothing was impossible for Him. Maybe not necessarily a total healing overnight, but in His time and His way. I was always overdosed, so even if medicine were His decision, He'd find the right one.

Another angel I met that first night came up and asked if she could pray for me. Dorothea was also a victim with uncontrolled seizures and God brought her directly to me that evening. She had a beautiful, sweet smile and said I could call her anytime. I couldn't understand how or why anyone who experienced seizures could have joy and be at peace praising the Lord. I would be mentored by her for many years as I had need for encouragement daily. She understood my need because she could relate to my illness. Her kindness and desire to help me melted my heart, which really was Jesus living in her that was prominent.

People at this church respected me and really cared for me. They sang scripture over and over and that made it easier to memorize them. The church was enveloped with angels. I always was offered rides to their homes or Bible studies so I could get out of the house. My kids now had friends to play with and life was getting beautiful again. I now had hope for healing which encouraged me to reach out and trust Jesus.

The pastors at the church prayed with me, shared wisdom and helped me find Jesus in a more personal way.

I always was asked if I needed anything, all I needed to do was ask, which opened more doors to get to know many more in the church. Roger was thrilled for me because I had friends who enjoyed being with me and helping whenever possible. No one at the other church even cared to chat with me. They had their cliques and I was treated as a nobody.

Many of the women were in a group called Women's Aglow. It is now Aglow International, because God chose to have the men of God partners in the worldwide ministry. They all desired to be part of my life, a shelter for comfort. Passion overflowed, and they became family to me. They still are close prayer warrior friends today.

Angel Lou Ann lived three blocks away from our new house. God had chosen the area where Lou Ann lived because He knew she would minister to me. Her children were our kids' ages, so they now had neighborhood friends. We chose to walk there daily for activity after lunch. She never said I don't have time today or I'm busy. Her door was always open. Looking back, I can see now why I couldn't stay away from her! Jesus lived in her heart and I wanted what she had!

Many of the women from this new church on Sunday nights did not work outside the home. They desired my friendship and as we grew closer, I realized other people had testing in their lives also, so I learned to get my focus off myself and unto others. They invited me to Bible studies in their homes, Aglow monthly meetings, luncheons or shopping. I was never alone.

Roger was elated, for now he knew I had real friends who enjoyed being with me just because of their love and desire to be used by God for His purposes. God had specifically chosen each one, who would be there, just for me.

How blessed I was with these angels! Do I ever remember saying thank you to them? I am not sure, but most likely not. Now is my opportunity to say thank you to all of my special angels!

Chapter 11

In the Swimming Pool

FOR SOME UNKNOWN reason, I received a call from angel Laura. She announced that someone had given her my name and told her I liked to swim. She lived a few blocks away and swam at the County Health Care's heated pool. She asked if I would be interested. How awesome is that? Winters days in Wisconsin lasted forever without a car to get out. I had gained weight in pregnancy and exercise outside was almost impossible with ice and snow.

Laura had close friends her age who came to the pool for exercise every week. I now had more new friends who would be compared to a mother-image for me. They were aware and ready to reach out in love. I needed a doctor's written permission stating therapy was necessary for my health. No problem. Amazing how God places caring angels in your life.

Unfortunately, I had a seizure in the shallow water of the pool. The lifeguards weren't watching, but God arranged for the pool administrator to walk in at that moment and spot me going under. He jumped in and rescued me! I was taken to the hospital. God will never leave or forsake you. The lifeguards were fired and now two guards would sit at the edge of the pool in case another emergency would occur again.

God's Hand of protection surrounded me wherever I went without me uttering a word.

This was the same therapy pool where I had taught Lori to swim after her terrible traffic accident, and my self-worth was renewed. I had the privilege of becoming an angel to someone else! She was paralyzed from the neck down and water therapy could restore her muscles. She was afraid of water but trusted me and let go of fear.

Talk about gutsy for me and her! Water therapy restored her muscles and enlightened me at the same time. I could see purpose for my trial because I now could reach out in love to help someone in great need. The door opened and I walked right through!

With daily therapy for many months, she was able to stand, tread water, use a walker, and finally a cane. And then one Sunday morning at church she surprised everyone by letting go and walking up the steps to the altar for communion. She was set free to walk on her own!

Chapter 12

Angels as Physicians

GOD HAD SPECIFIC PLANS WRITTEN for me. He knew exactly which doctor I would need in every circumstance. After the ordeal with encephalitis and the three angelic Jewish doctors in Chicago, He had created others for my parents and Roger to be aware of when more health issues arose. Sad to say, I would be in great need frequently.

After the river accident, Dr. David, our family doctor, would be a special key player in my new-found life with seizures. He cared a lot for me and our family and wanted only the best for us. He would later take care of my mom who eventually moved up to Wisconsin from Venice, Fla., after my dad passed away.

When we moved to central Wisconsin, it was a challenge finding a specialist in neurology. Pharmacies also had very few drugs in the early '70s that would work for my type seizures. So, it became a guessing game as to what to try and more importantly what were the challenging side-effects going to be.

It was actually quite scary and disappointing as we walked for years with no medications doing anything to calm the seizures. All the doctors could do was to increase the dose to try to contain the severity and frequency of the seizures. We would find out many years later that overdosing was just as damaging as not having enough medicine in your system.

Angel Dr. David was always available to see us and opened appointments when there were none available. He directed us to many specialists, and labs were always busy drawing blood with frequent visits. After over 16 years of seizures and continual overdosing and switching medicines with every new doctor we saw, I finally shared a concern with Roger. "Why do I see two of everything on the television screen?" Roger was shocked.

My long-time neurologist seemed to think overdosing would work. She refused to refer or even send information to any other doctor in the area we lived in. She was arrogant and proud, and definitely *not* an angel. She thought she had all the answers and wanted to be the doctor who would get the glory for my healing. Dr. David heard about this, stepped in and faxed my medical records to the Marshfield Clinic in Marshfield, Wis., which is part of the famous Mayo Clinic in Rochester, Minn.

We had an appointment the next day with the head of the neurology department God again provided another great angel, Dr. Kevin, to keep me under His wing and safe inside His arms of love. We expected many hours of long tests and eventually results would show the safest, most effective choice we had. To our surprise, Dr. Kevin simply asked me walk a straight line to the wall and back to him. He looked directly into my eyes and said no tests were necessary. He said my double vision came as a result of very high amounts of medication, a triple overdose!

We were amazed and knew right away why Dr. David sent us to him. He told us it would take time to accurately know for certain what correct amount of medicine would be to stop seizure activity. We could not just stop the large amounts of drugs overnight; it had to be very gradual. Within six months the levels were close to the correct amount necessary, but seizure activity continued. We had one alternative. This clinic specialized in drug studies. Would

I be willing to try a not-yet-FDA-approved medication? I could be given a placebo drug or the real thing.

After waiting over 16 years, I truly didn't care what might happen and what did I have to lose? I signed ominous forms stating, "If you die, they were not responsible." I may have reacted too quickly, but I was ready for adventure. As soon as I took the new medicine the very next morning, I knew this was not a placebo.

It was the real thing, because my legs were weak and I felt dizzy when trying to walk a straight line. Being part of this study would be quite a challenge. I decided to keep going forward, trusting this could be my miracle drug.

So, God had opened a door for healing because we were willing to take a chance to see if it would help. Had we stayed with the small-town doctor, I never would have had the privilege given to me to try and see if this would work. This new medication would now set me free and bring new life into me.

I was blessed finding another special angel, Dr. Samir, my obstetrician and gynecologist. He performed a partial hysterectomy at age 40, having found cancer cells. Another angel surgeon, Dr. Sally, cut out a small cyst on my rib cage and found breast cancer. She removed close to 20 lymph nodes. The oncologist we saw ordered chemo for three months and 29 days of radiation following the chemo.

While living in cooler, drier Wisconsin, my lymph nodes that regulate fluids in my affected arm functioned well. However, in humid Florida, my arm swelled all the time. I am trusting God will heal it in His time. Until then, I have therapy and I use a custom-made arm sleeve with Velcro to keep the swelling down. God can heal instantly or He can use equipment made just for my needs.

When I had my hips replaced, I thought the local surgeon could qualify as an angel but now I am not sure. We trusted the orthopedic surgeon who operated on both hips, just a few years apart, using the posterior approach. He was known for his ability to make small incisions versus 10 inches. It could heal faster. We found out a few years later that he was using hip sockets that had already been recalled and did not share this with his patients.

The recall occurred because the metal sockets rubbed against each other when exercising, causing cobalt and chromium particles to flow directly into the blood system. The poisons were being released more quickly in younger, more active people than in elderly folks. The principal side effect of cobalt poisoning was seizures. I was a perfect victim. There was a major lawsuit suing the hip replacement company, in which we eventually received a settlement.

My brother Tom, another angel in disguise, personally knew an orthopedic surgeon who worked at his hospital. Tom sent us to Austin, Texas, to meet his friend, Dr. Dave, an angel for sure. He was able to replace both hip sockets together at the same time because of my age and good health. He would use the anterior approach, which heals very quickly because they cut one small incision versus two deeper incisions.

They finish the surgery using glue and staples. Water therapy was used five days right after the double hip procedure. They just put tape over the incisions and I walked right into the pool. I floated and was buoyant so no pain was felt while exercising. Doctors then can remove the staples and we flew home. However, although the incision was smaller and healed more quickly, the nerve damage was severe for about three months. No complications arose and I was again set fee.

Only God knew what doctors I would need, when, and in which town we'd find them. We could trust God totally through all major accidents or illnesses. Good doctors are hard to find in special fields and I will, as well as my whole family, be forever grateful for all the referrals and knowledge given to us over the years.

CHAPTER 13

Four-legged Angels

MANY PEOPLE MAY not see the blessings and benefits of holding or cradling a warm furry body when you need something to hold onto when no one else was around. It doesn't take much to make them happy and they are special angels, disguised in fur. Some angels don't have wings, they have four paws, soft furry bodies and unconditional love.

I consider our two cats special angels. Our first cat, Boo Boo, was a sweetheart and had the patience of a saint. He was initially a garage cat when our son brought him home. He was a Maine coon breed with long fur that matted. He was there for me 24/7 and had great listening ears. I could cry, scream or be angry and it never bothered him. What a blessing! He never walked away and was always in the room I occupied.

For over 16 years with seizures, I needed a companion by my side. Icy, long, cold winters caused a lot of indoor activity for me. Boo Boo and I had fun together sewing, painting walls and ripping wallpaper off the walls. He brought lots of laughter and joy and relieved the loneliness.

Boo Boo was an indoor cat who loved getting outside. I got lots of exercise chasing him back in the house. He kept me slim and fit. He was adorable and loved being on top of me whenever I sat down. He was a people cat and very loving.

After Boo Boo passed away, we got Lexie, who belonged to our daughter in college and still is a constant companion today. She never leaves my side. She is always caring, adorable and knows what to do to get attention. Either on her back up-side-down with her feet up or howling until we play with her favorite toy she drags all over the house since she was a small kitty.

We always know she will greet us anytime we've been gone from home because she is a social butterfly. She listens and then decides what she will do. She never tells me to go away and likes being cuddled and starts purring.

I am not sure why some people do not like cats. Allergies would be a good reason. They are always fun and bring laughter. Many friends and occasional cat sitters agree that Lexie is a unique cat and fun to watch. She is definitely independent and makes her own decisions as to when she has had enough. She has seen many tears run down my face and knows when I need comforting.

I'm sure she knows all the words to many songs because music is always on. She likes Florida weather better than the cold Wisconsin climate. She loves the lanai though it gets very hot and humid at times. She is always contented, natural and joyful to have around.

Our grandkids love Lexie and now are blessed with a cat of their own. We are known as the "kitty" grandma and grandpa. I am saddened now as I watch my precious furry love bug, as she struggles with health issues in her senior years.

God knew I needed Boo Boo and Lexie, both priceless four-legged angels, each one of a kind. I feel blessed having both cats at different times in my life close by my side, on my lap or on our bed all night.

Chapter 14

My Support Groups

WHEN YOU HAVE a disability, nothing is better than knowing or meeting someone who is aware of the conditions you are living in. No one has to wonder or guess. We all have something in common, and have compassionate ears and know how to uplift each other when hurting abides inside.

I was introduced to special friends who are special angels in disguise. The epilepsy support group had members who were easy to love. We all went on epilepsy strolls together and had monthly meetings and picnics that everyone enjoyed while sharing your thoughts, hopes and dreams. We all needed encouragement and enjoyed sharing excitement when someone in the group was blessed finding a drug that set them free.

Nearly everyone with a disability seemed to have peace in their hearts, because they had Jesus as a best friend. I was able to bring hope to encourage others because there was a drug study going on that I was involved in and it had been my miracle drug.

At this time angel Marilyn heard about my doctor and called me. She introduced herself by sharing the fact that she also had seizures. She was not able to drive, but I was able to help her meet my doctor. He referred her to a surgeon who performed successful brain surgery. She gave others in the group hope knowing that in some cases surgery was a possible route to healing.

Seizures were not the problem for any of us. It was the loss of freedom and total dependence on others for transportation anywhere for any need.

My breast cancer support group had a few friends who needed each other to share stories with. One young girl came to a meeting on a cold rainy night. God planned for me to be there, you might say a divine appointment. Denise and I were the only ones who braved the storm. It was just the two of us there. I could tell she was scared and shy. She had stage four breast cancer and was refusing chemotherapy.

What a blessing that I showed up for her. I was able to share what happened to me and let her know I really had no side effects like she'd read and heard. It gave her confidence that she now would go and do it. I walked through it all with her. Her family was thrilled I had stepped into her life at the right time, because she could have died at a very young age. She was a special gift that opened up many doors, knowing victims really needed to see hope in the flesh.

While walking through breast cancer myself, I really needed someone I could confide in who really had strong faith. After all I had come through as a victor, I have no idea why I was afraid of chemotherapy and radiation treatments. Fear is wicked. Your mind runs in all directions, and once a thought develops, it travels everywhere. I needed an angel who could help me walk through a fire so I could grow closer to Jesus and fear would disappear. I needed the angel in some form I could see and whose hand I could hold onto.

Yes, I had Roger and Jesus, but I also needed a human angel. Someone whose eyes I could see and was available for a shoulder to cry on. That's when angel Sharon appeared, who had caring, listening ears and could understand my emotional needs. Sharon was the wife of one of Roger's co-workers and worked in hospice, where she was patient, kind and compassionate.

Thank God I was never aware of setbacks and problems chemo and radiation could bring. I really was like Denise with a fear of the unknown. Sharon came daily to sit and chat, knowing I needed it. She chose to come on her own. When you have gone through a great deal of anguish yourself, it becomes natural to you. You are totally aware of others' needs as the Holy Spirit provides insight.

Her sweet, gentle voice of assurance, encouraged me to hold on and bite the bullet. Roger was speechless when it came to really understanding my emotional needs. God had me in the palm of His hands. She brought peace to me, even though I saw the challenges I'd be facing. The word cancer is nasty. People need others desperately while experiencing confusion and fear.

God put Sharon there for me to realize I'd be okay. I'd get to ring the victory bell with joy in the doctors' office, declaring I had fought the fight and finished the race. The poisons had killed all the cancer cells and I was set free. I needed His grace and mercy which He provided through a kind, generous, angelic friend who really loved Jesus and personally cared about me.

CHAPTER 15

Christopher and Elizabeth

CONSIDERING THE FACT that the doctors said "no" to our having children and if we had listened to them, our lives would have been very different and totally empty. I am so glad we decided to do it our way. As I said earlier, we were first blessed with Christopher and four years later, with Elizabeth. They were both easy pregnancies and deliveries.

Having children while on anti-convulsant medications was a major cause for concern. Birth defects were possible. We trusted God that they would be healthy and strong. God was in control and helped us walk through many trials and He always had open doors for us to walk through as He directed us to doctors with great wisdom.

As Chris and Liz grew older they were aware of dangers that could happen when I had a seizure. They had watched their disabled mom for years as I'd fall. They were always on the lookout and never really knew exactly what to do if an emergency occurred. They learned to just watch and try not to help. There was nothing they could do to stop it.

My angel children had become strong and brave on their own. They loved me unconditionally. I came to admire their courage, fortitude and ability to handle stressful situations. My illness had prepared them to walk an extra mile to reach out for anyone who had any disability. There are many needy people in this fallen world. It helped mold them into who they are today.

There seemed to be no hope for a cure to stop the seizures. Then they witnessed what I call an angelic intervention! I was accepted for the drug study in Marshfield, Wis. There another angel appeared, Ginny, an old college buddy, who happened to live in this small farm town. She offered me a ride home so Roger could just drop me off and she'd bring me home after my appointments and of course, shopping and lunch.

There was nothing I had to be ashamed of; seizures just happened. The kids and I never talked about it. It was just a way of life. I regret never really being aware of what went on in their heads as the years rolled by. Roger had a closer relationship with them. There were many times, I'm sure, that they may have discussed my illness and how they felt or what may have happened from remarks of witnesses walking by as I fell.

All things work together for good to those who love God and are called according to his purpose for them. I don't think fear was ever an issue, but it may have been. I am truly amazed how they were able to handle their lives as challenges continued for my brave angels.

There would always be a continual thought pattern bouncing around in my mind daily. Did I take my medication or forget it? And the timing was always crucial. These concerns are never forgotten and became a natural way of life as days turned into decades.

Traveling with family we'd watch out for one another. Pill popping actually became a game and a challenge while traveling overseas, as we'd pass over five or six time zones!

I usually kept my watch in our original time zone and then planned how far apart each one should be, just to be safe. Most of the time we figured it out without having a problem with surprise seizures.

My whole family was always on alert, and this continues to this day. I guess it was really a puzzle to figure out just who was taking care of whom. I can always say I was there caring for my kids but it was also them caring for mom. It was really a different upbringing. I am grateful for all the love that surrounded me.

I can only imagine the chaos that was created for everyone as a seizure occurred, and how quickly they had to react so I would remain unharmed. I think it might have been interesting to just see a rerun of the whole drama that was lived out as I fell and slowly came back to life. Then again, I really don't think I'd want to.

I consider both children gifts from God. As they were growing up, there were many unusual trials they'd experience that most children would never see. They had to be brave and just take over as needed. God created them to be ready, willing and able in all circumstances, to just jump in and take over. I have no idea what went on in their heads, but they were always prepared to reach out in love.

I remember Liz telling me we were waiting to check out at the grocery store one day, a seizure came on, and I fell hard. She was able to get me up off the floor, into our car and off to the emergency room. As I was coming out of the seizure after about 10 minutes, I said my wrist hurt. Our fears were confirmed: I had broken my wrist.

She told me what happened. I was never ashamed or embarrassed, but amazed at her diligence to just take over without fear. She knew exactly what needed to be done and did it. God blessed Roger and me with wonderful, compassionate, and caring children. Never a dull moment, but life kept going on and new adventures continued daily.

Roger was never truly aware what went on while he was at work. He just trusted Jesus that the kids would be safe when I was semiconscious after a seizure. I truly believe they saw the love their dad had for me. It became "a learn by watching" experience to see how they should react in time of need.

There were many times I was sad and felt empty inside while they were growing up. I never could drive them to their friends' homes or to after-school activities. But as time passes, I can see they learned to cope with hardships, and it made them strong and developed a desire for them to reach out and help those in need.

God allowed this season of their lives to help them mature and develop skills as caregivers. It was amazing to see God move in their lives, making them capable of handling anything at a moment's notice. They always had big hearts, especially for handicapped friends or folks we'd meet who were in need of help.

CHAPTER 16

God's Purpose Revealed

THOUGH I COULDN'T see it at the time, John 9:3 states, "This happened so the power of God could be seen in him." God can use disability to show His goodness and power. I was told no matter what my condition was, to honor God with it. Suffering can cause the blame game, causing you to look back at an irresponsible act, like my shallow dive and actually believe you were being punished for doing such a dumb thing.

God wove his heart's concern and tender care for those with disabilities. His compassion for those affected with disability did not stand out because it was already a part of his plan for his people. Scripture gives us insight into his provision and protection of people with disabilities.

As the Creator, God assumes responsibility for disabilities. God is not the cause, but the enabler and final rescuer of handicapped people. To say God is responsible for disability is different from the serious mistake of blaming God for it. Exodus 4:11 states, "Who makes a person's mouth? Who decides whether people speak or do not speak, hear or do not hear, see or do not see? Is it not I, the Lord?" He will provide for the needs for his people.

As God's creatures, we groan with pain and sadness for disability to be healed. Regardless of how blessed we appear, we are still in pain this side of heaven.

Many people are surprised to discover God's plan for people with handicaps was not only to glorify Jesus through miraculous healings, but also that they would minister to others, not just in their own disabilities, but because of them. People affected by disability serve others in many ways, but the most prominent way is through their obvious need of support from others. Disabled people allow Jesus to show compassion, to bring God glory and to demonstrate His place as God's Son, the Messiah.

Finally, by healing people with disabilities, Jesus demonstrated that He is God. People with handicaps give Jesus an opportunity to correct a number of wrong ideas about God's love and about human suffering. He allows disabilities for His good purposes: to bring glory to Himself, spiritual growth in people with disabilities, and ministry opportunity and blessings for believers who serve the disability community.

The Bible teaches that we should pray according to God's will and God will do what He has planned, which may or may not include healing. When Jesus returns at His second coming, He will bring justice to those who have disabilities, activate hope and reward the faithful. The end of God's story of disability will be a new beginning.

Perfect bodies, perfect minds, and perfect praise for our God, whose story has always included disability. No wonder John tells us that God will wipe away every tear from our eyes and we will sing a new song. No wonder he concludes with a prayer from Revelation 22:20, "Amen! Come, Lord Jesus!"

People with disabilities actually have something eternally precious in common with Christ in His suffering. There is a sweet union that sickness has forged between us and Jesus. In heaven I will not praise the suffering, but praise the wisdom and power of God in using my seizures to drive me directly home to Him.

Chapter 17

The Little Angels

I JUST KNOW BEYOND the shadow of a doubt that God had our children created just for us before the world began. They were created for our pleasure and angels delivered each one of them as angels. Granted, there were days they did not behave as angels should but nevertheless, angels.

Grandchildren are totally amazing and true gifts God creates just to bless us. We have an awesome God! Angels delivered all of them directly to us at no cost. A great surprise and joy.

I had shared earlier that our doctors said very firmly, do not have children because of my need for safety and my health problems. Roger said I was stubborn. Yes, he was right, but he also wanted children. Sometimes it seems to be a good thing to occasionally disagree with him and do your own thing.

Many times, their advice has been very good especially when safety was an issue. They did have deep concern. However, when you are 27 and not able to teach school anymore, I thought: what else is there for me to do with my long, never-ending days? It seemed a natural thing to do and we were excited for something good to happen.

When Christopher was born and very healthy, we were thrilled we were blessed by God Himself. We have enjoyed parenthood. Elizabeth was another great gift and we were grateful we had two beautiful children. Yes, there were setbacks with my health issues, but through it all we survived.

Now let me tell you about our four little angels, our grandchildren. Madelyn is 12 and doing well in everything she tries out for and she is always ready for more. We enjoy special time with her and can carry on great conversations about almost anything. She is a great big sister and teaches her sisters many games and is so patient with both of them

Madelyn blessed me by reading my first book, *Sink or Swim?*, and shared it with her teacher, which was special. I think she enjoyed finding out more about her grandma in Florida, which was great because we never had a lot of time sharing thoughts, feelings and ideas before because we lived too far away. She is very sensitive and has a sweet personality like her mom.

Violet, eight years old, is one of a kind. She is her very own special self, full of surprises and fun. Whenever there is a game or contest, she is always out to win. She was selling Girl Scout cookies and opened her own web site and sold over 700 boxes of cookies on line. Whenever a challenge comes her way, she will pursue it and keep marching forward.

Violet enjoys making people laugh and playing center stage. There is also a very serious side to her, which is full of love and compassion for others. She shares deep feelings and emotions and expresses herself with love hugs and smiles. She has a lot of personality traits like her dad.

Graycen is four years old and always full of surprises. She has a very creative mind and is always making up games and has rules and plans for all to follow. She enjoys fun and is a good teacher with great ideas. She has a quiet side to her and thinks things through and listens carefully and will tell you exactly what she's thinking about and shares her ideas using lots of wisdom for her age.

Graycen has a great memory and always thinking one step ahead of everyone. She has a deep thought process and amazing things just pop out of her mouth that are either funny or quite serious. She loves people and loves to crawl into your arms and fall asleep. She also can tell people just how she feels and what she is thinking, which can be very astounding. Her beautiful spirit is half mom and half dad.

Maribella seems older than age two. She has her own personality which is always expressed in some form or another. Who ever heard of a toddler giving herself a timeout? She did! She is a fast learner and talks well as she expresses herself. She sings nursery rhymes and counts to 10 in Spanish.

Maribella has her own mind and enjoys playing by herself or with others at playgrounds or school. She runs to be hugged by all who know and love her. She is a combination of her mother, our daughter, and her dad. God is full of grace, mercy and love. It will be great joy seeing her blossom into her own unique person God created her to be.

Our children and their spouses are all great parents. They love and spend time with their children and do whatever they can to help them grow and mature each year. They are consistent in discipline and desire to help them find out who they really are and what they would enjoy doing when they grew into adulthood.

Traveling and seeing them in their homes or on vacation, and babysitting when parents leave town is always fun and sometimes a challenge, but worth every worn out, stretched muscle and lack of sleep. It is a great way to bring us all into a closer a relationship, getting to know each other like never before. Life is shorter than we realize and time with family is precious.

Our families are far apart but when we do come together, our time is so special. The smiles, giggles and hugs are worth a million dollars! Everyone grows up too fast, so we must make great efforts to come together whenever a door opens. Close-knit families are so blessed. If we had listened to the doctors, look at what we would have missed! I can't imagine life without these precious gifts of life, these little angels.

CHAPTER 18

My Beloved Roger

I HAVE SHARED many memories throughout this book of just how Roger has blessed me throughout our married lives and will always continue to care until Jesus calls me home.

There isn't a day that I can say for certain, "I can handle this one all by myself." Other strong, capable people take full responsibility for my daily care and have just made their lives envelop totally around my being. I am able to drive again, but it is a major concern as I pull out of the driveway. They can only ask me so many times, "Did you take your meds or are you too stressed to be going anywhere right now?"

It is freedom for me and a blessed privilege to have my desire fulfilled so I can share my life experiences with others. People are never really aware of how blessed they are to be able to get into a car and take off. Seizures were never the problem, but it was the continual need to keep asking for a ride, not just from friends but from Roger too.

If God wants me to get somewhere, I can drive. However, if my medicines are not balanced, I depend totally on Roger, a close friend or neighbor to help me get where I need to go. I walk out each day also trusting I can remember taking pills as alarms go off, but sometimes I even mess that up.

Roger listens and obeys His plan as best as a human mind can. He has to trust and have faith that God has me in His hands alone. One day at a time is all anyone can handle. I consider every day a gift and only He has the days of my life planned until He chooses to say, "come home."

It truly is amazing to see how God knew Roger would meet me and we'd know He had arranged our meeting and His timing was perfect.

Surely, we have many differences, but they say opposites attract. I can think in a completely different way in many circumstances that are in complete opposition to his thoughts, but our lives together are very special and we feel blessed.

There were many times it seemed situations would not ever work out, especially while raising our children. We both came from completely different backgrounds and his parents were complete opposites from mine. We both were disciplined differently, as his parents were strict and rule-oriented, and mine were more laid back and open to change.

I am truly amazed as to the incredible amounts of stress and the uncertainty of how things might turn out. I never had much experience caring for any close-knit family members and never realized how circumstances can catch you unawares. Roger and I were able to care for our mothers while they lived in nursing homes. We enjoyed giving them comfort and uplifting their spirits by just being there.

Roger is now experiencing a physical battle of his own with ongoing eye surgeries. It is very stressful to watch a close loved one in pain and help the best you can. But maybe I am his angel? I hope so. Now he needs me as I needed him in times of trial.

I think back now as to how Roger never complained and kept walking through years of trials. He held on tightly as a husband should, trusting that God had a plan and he would follow it. I am amazed at how he was able to concentrate on his job and come home and take me to doctor appointments, and discipline the children. He held our family together under stressful situations. This is what I call a totally dedicated man with a full desire to hold us together despite the circumstances,

God chose Roger to represent His love. God knew Roger would remain faithful to me through sickness and health and it would not be easy. In fact, he has said that, "I promised I would be with you no matter what happened and I meant it." Roger, my angel in disguise, chose to be ready for anything. There has never been a dull moment for the last 46 years and counting.

Not many men would have desired to stay in dire circumstances and remain strong and devoted to me as we walked day by day through many fires and many years having no idea what could arise. God was never going to let go of Roger or me. God gave me angels on assignment throughout my whole life. Roger played the strong role model of how to handle struggles and be content with whatever God had planned. We both learned just to let go and trust God.

Chapter 19

God's Great Love

GOD CREATED MANY angels for me and for every other human being that He created because he loves us so much.

The book of First Corinthians in chapter 13 tells everyone all about love.

"If I speak in tongues of men and Angels and have no love, I am only a resounding gong or clanging cymbal.

"If I have the gift of prophecy and can fathom all mysteries and all knowledge, and if I have a faith that can move mountains, but have not love, I am nothing.

"If I give all I possess to the poor and surrender my body to the flames, but have not love, I gain nothing.

"Love is patient and kind. It does not envy, it does not boast, it is not proud. It is not rude, it is not self-seeking, it is not easily angered, it keeps no records of wrongs.

"Love does not delight in evil , but rejoices with the truth. It always protects, always trusts, always hopes, always perseveres. Love never fails.

"But where there are prophecies, they will cease; where there are tongues, they will be stilled; where there is knowledge, it will pass away.

"For we know in part and we prophecy in part, but when perfection comes, the imperfect disappears.

"Now we see but a poor reflection as in a mirror; then we shall see face to face. Now I know in part; then I shall know fully, even as I am fully known.

"And now these three remain, faith, hope and love. But the greatest of these is love."

Everything anyone did for my family or me was motivated purely by love. They all had great faith and a sincere desire to reach out and touch our family. They gave our family hope and encouragement for many years.

They were full of love in their hearts and had a great desire to go full speed ahead no matter what the cost. We never had to think about asking anyone to assist us, because God was the Master designer and knew who would be there at a moment's notice. Angels in disguise and angels I never saw, whom I call guardian angels, were a total blessing then and still are today.

Conclusion

On Looking Back

THIS TERM, "LOOKING back" was always something we were told not to do. We were always told don't dwell in the past, but look forward only to your future. They always made it sound so terrible, but it also can be totally helpful and amazing!

I can now say, if I hadn't looked back, I never would have seen all the great miracles God performed in my life. Angels performed continually as God put them in place and always at the right time.

Seeing miracles before your eyes as days turned into years, you can only wonder what the purpose of anything you may think was totally unnecessary and then God turns it around only for good (Romans 8:28).

So yes, I could say, "What if I hadn't done the stupid shallow dive but that stupid dive helped make me who I am today." It also made Roger, my parents, doctors, friends, children and anyone who knew me who they are today, because we all learn and can be blessed just because the experience existed.

I could look at my life and wonder why didn't God just take me home? I have imagined myself as a burden to every person I met. He is the Potter and we are the clay. He molds and makes us into His own Image and sometimes that hurts. But whatever He allows, there is a reason for it.

Seizures allowed me to be who I am today and also molded my caregivers into His workmanship and all who are blessed with life, grow stronger in faith through testing. They all could have said to God, "We've had it and can't handle Jane's illness. We are too busy and it takes too much of our day. There must be someone else who has more experience, because we really don't know what to do."

Where would I be? But God chose specific angels who would step up to the plate and say, "Count me in!" They had this desire built in to their hearts and chose to reach out in love because that was the way God created them. It took great courage for them to say as Isaiah 6:8 states, "Here am I, send me!"

The creation of each human being didn't just happen in the simple snap of God's finger. There is a song that states, "mold me, make me, fill me and use me." When He created each one of us, He had a destiny in place as to what He would allow and permit in each of our lives to make us more like Him.

I believe looking back opens doors of things you may never have seen. It opens our minds to seeing His purposes come forth when initially we could see nothing. Sure, a dumb dive, a triple overdose, car accidents, illnesses and surgeries, they were not only planned prior to my birth, but God allowed them to occur.

My life would open up new avenues for people who were really not aware of their purpose for living. People just opened up their hearts without realizing what would be happening when they said yes to reaching out in love. They would learn to be more like Jesus in their actions, doing things they'd never tried before.

Yes, I am an overcomer. I could be wrestling with the mysteries of suffering and pain and then look at God's sovereignty. What could have been His purpose? God calls His people, His treasure (Deuteronomy 26:18).

In Matthew 18:10, Jesus speaks of God the Father giving special attention to the needs of "little ones." This phrase refers to children, but it also includes everyone who might be categorized as one of the "least of these" (Matthew 25:40). The chronically ill, disabled, mentally ill, all those who are unable to care for themselves or provide for their own needs. God especially treasures these.

He has given us the responsibility to care for those He considers his special treasure. Whether we have been charged with the care of a physically disabled person, or and elderly person in a nursing home, every believer has a part to play. Though we may experience fear or feel we aren't able to handle the circumstances, we can take comfort in knowing that God is protecting us and will save all his treasured people.

Having experienced walking in fires of uncontrolled seizure activity and breast cancer, I have learned how to minister or mentor others who are involved with these handicaps, because God used my disabilities to reach out in love to those who had need. Am I an angel to these people? I believe it was God's intent.

Patience is a gift which can be hard to handle. Waiting for God to make the first move can be very difficult. I have learned His timing is always perfect. Surely, it would be easier to get it over with and get on to the next phase, but while you are deep in the valley, you realize from past experiences, there will always be a mountaintop.

That alone gives you hope and courage, knowing you can make it. I guess you could say, you can see the light at the end of the tunnel. God is sovereign and knows how much you can handle (1 Corinthians 10:13).

To my dismay, I have tried my own way, thinking it was a great idea and then later realized, I should have accepted the discipline I needed, and to just let go of my own plan. You can cause delay by steering the opposite way instead of His Way. It may seem difficult at the time, but His way is the only way.

If it weren't for His angels having charge over me, encouraging and uplifting me, and helping me know I could make it, I never could be where I am now. Praise the Lord, clap your hands, shout unto God with a voice of triumph! He has done great and mighty acts and is full of love for everyone.